Through The
Storm

COLETTE GRANT

ISBN: 978-1-955312-36-3

Printed in the United States of America
Story Corner Publishing & Consulting, Inc.
1510 Atlanta Ave.
Portsmouth, VA 23704

Storycornerpublishing@yahoo.com
www.StoryCornerPublishing.com

Dedication

This book is for an amazing queen who has been my best friend through some of the most challenging times in my life. Ms. Liesa Day, thank you for always being there for me! Without your love and encouragement, this book may have never been written and shared with the world. Gratitude turns what we have into enough and more! Denial turns into acceptance, chaos into order, confusion into clarity when you are near. With you in my life, our past makes sense and brings peace for today, and creates a vision for tomorrow.

Continue to be you and let people see the real, imperfect, flawed, quirky, weird, beautiful, and magical person you are. I am forever thankful for you! I even adore all the parts of you that sometimes you may forget to love. Thank you for being a special person in my life who gave me the confidence to believe that my story wasn't over! Ms. Liesa Day, I dedicate this book to you.

Table Of Content

Introduction

The one smiling cry alone at night.
The strongest person is actually the weakest one.
The brave man is the most scared on the inside.
The famous one is lonely all the time.
People are so different from what they portray.
There are so many emotions people hide,
Some people may act as if they are tough,
But maybe they are already at their breaking point.
Who knows that the laughing manic next to you cries all night?
Not everyone is as strong and brave as they show their weakness.
Don't let the outer mask confound you.
A smile can lie, but the eyes can't.
Look deep into the eyes, and maybe you can save a soul from breaking.

This book is a summation of real-life poetry. Take a look at life through my eyes for a moment and tell me what you see. Understand situations can change. All you must do is believe.

Self-Identification:
Death of My Generation

A self-destructing generation has ignored the definition of
individuality. The youth lack preparation. The elders lack to
educate. Instead of motivation, they limit the growth of a dying
child, and it's devastating. They put on makeup to fake a persona
that's made up. Quick pic selfies and quick flicks. We live through
social standards, thinking that things will be alright. Imagination
and fairytale insight. That is very much real. You can't put a filter
on life.

Man child, boys who won't grow into men because they weren't
taught to walk in faith. We are ruined with sin. The beauty of
a woman has lost its value. Time is not on our side. With every
passing hour, a piece of my generation dies. My heart cries for
answers. Maybe it's a double standard, but it's the cold truth.
Acceptance is the first step to solving a problem. We have too many
children and not enough fathers. We have so many issues, but why

bother. They say the projects is a project. Experimentation, I call it. We are like crabs in a barrel. We bring each other down. Look in the mirror. You find your worst enemy. I have yet to fathom the entirety of the world's pain, again the lack of self-definition.

Suppose we don't define ourselves, then society will. Guns are a must, and books are a bust. We put our hope in men when it should be in God, who we should trust as this dying generation begs for resuscitation. I see the hands around their necks, and I witness suffocation. Before I die, I have one last statement we as a people must stop the justification of defacing the generation. Will you fight for the right to stand tall, or will you fall, fall victim to the brutal death of a dying generation?

Growing up, we often allow life's circumstances to define who we are. We begin to let our minds think that this is our life and there's no coming back from it. Well, allow me to correct that notion. We all encounter storms, but it's about pressing our way through. Throughout these pages, I will express some of my own experiences and encouragement. I hope to assure you that where you come from and what you've been through doesn't have to make you! We all have trials and tribulations that we must endure. With support, we don't have to fight those battles alone. In a world that profits from every self-doubt you make, I hope you realize your life is not theirs to dictate. I guess the cost of living a life that's not yours is knowing you had a disease for which you carried the cure. By doing what you love, you'll automatically attract like-minded people and lose the rest. Live the life you want, and all else will fall into place.

Stare at the sky every day, hoping paths will cross for you and change lives. Give life to hearts that were once blue, but only when you realize the whole universe has waited for the beginning of you. You must believe you were destined for great things!!!

Self-doubt is defined as a lack of confidence in oneself and abilities. In life, we endure dark times, and when we go through these times, our self-image changes. As a child, I had many bad experiences. As time progressed, I let those occurrences dictate who I was becoming. They begin to control me. Too often, we allow ourselves to linger in dark places, thinking that this is how it has to be. When in actuality, we have the power to change reality.

We may not change past events, but we sure don't have to let the past shape our future. Often, we envision where we want to be in life. When fear surfaces, it tends to hold us back from our goals and dreams. When fear takes over, it may be hard to shake, and you begin to believe you can't overcome your obstacles. Fortunately, that's not true. You have to tell yourself that they were steppingstones to your future, but they don't have to destroy you. You must let them shape you into being better, elevate your thoughts in a positive light. Sometimes we get caught up in what we see during the storm and not how we survived it.

You must reclaim your life because you made it through. While you may have some battle scars, those scars represent the strength and fight in you. You can persevere and make it through anything if you believe in yourself. No, it won't be easy, but it will be worth it when you're able to look back to acknowledge your growth in overcoming the storm.

Dreams
of
Dreams

*L*aying lifeless. The breeze from the north caught me. Living in a city where taking the low road is taken so easily. You become a custom to a custom that's frowned upon these days. A broke man or woman with a millionaire's mindset is what they call it. The street uses you as bait. Another victim to a gun or a zombie to the drug game. Sleep soothes the pain. Your imagination helps you dream that dream. Intellect sets you apart, but your background puts you in the same bracket. You move forward to the triumphs that awaits, vowing never to look backward.

The dream you dreamt isn't as clear as before. It seems as if the soul points you in the direction of hope, but fate will not allow you to open that door. Repetition is the true foundation of knowledge. True ambition lies somewhere between faith and fear. True acceptance lies somewhere between serenity and rage. The dream can become a thought. That thought can become action, and that action becomes reality. A wise man once wrote if you do not stop you can become unstoppable. Dreams are vivid depictions of who we want to be. Become that in which you imagine. Don't let dreams just be!!

The mind is a beautiful thing because that's where a thought or notion begins. We sometimes start in a dark place, but we can't allow it to end there. You must elevate to change your mindset to get to where you want to be in life. When I was younger, I was depressed, and my mind reached extremely low depths and darkness due to what I endured as a child. I believed that I wouldn't amount to anything or experience true love because that's what I was fed. As kids, we expect our parents to keep us safe and guide us down the right path. However, that's not always reality. Often things they had experienced cause them to be complacent. Their minds become stuck on what they had been through. The truth is parenting doesn't come with a manual. We tend to play the blame game, looking for someone to pin our misfortune on. It's not about what you've been through. It's about how you rise to utilize all the bad to make you great. Don't allow a generational curse to hinder you from being great. You hold the power to triumph and break the cycle. Take a stand, break the chains, and fight for your future.

The circumstances don't have to hinder you. You must want more for your life, speaking from experience, trials can hold you back, but only if you allow it. Tell yourself you're worth more than your past. The storms you've been through can add value to your life, so use it as a testimony to help someone else. Reclaim your life! Don't be afraid to make a mistake because it shows that you're trying. You can do anything you set your mind to. No, it won't be easy but believe in yourself and it will definitely be worth it. Your past doesn't have to be your future! You survived it so you can get through anything.

I was assigned to move mountains, a structure larger and heavier than any other before. With a weak mind and ashen energy, I begin to push but with every thrust it swung back harder fragmentizing me to the solid ground. Below my hammered feet with frustration in my heart I settled crying until the tears ran dry and I could shed no more. It was a familiar voice that whispered in my ear reminding me that I have always been a great force. So, I chose to rise again standing tall, extracting the rusted spikes that controlled the measures of my movement with all the strength that I could muster. I began climbing, dragging myself along the side of impenetrable obstacles. Lacerated and sore, I remained vigilant with every passing day. I heave myself higher knowing that I will reach the apex where the view of the open prairie awaits my wild run. Someday I will rejoice. I will succeed, and I will conquer. I will never have to wear the shawl of weakness again!

Life is what you make of it. Your battles don't have to break you. If you have a vision, fight for it. The harder you fight the harder it may get but never give up. Hope is something that you're really going to have to hold on to fight through the tears and sleepless nights. If you don't fight for you, no one will! You have purpose and when the world grows dark and your soul feels heavy, raise up to meet the sky. Spend the night with infinity, let the universe wrap around you and love you. Let love pull your soul out of the darkness. Rest your head on hope and know that you are loved. Sometimes you may feel unworthy of love or as if you don't know what love is because you've never really felt it. Please know that you're worth it and you deserve every bit of love that is given to you. You must believe that! Let go of past events and find yourself even though you've been through the worst. It doesn't mean greatness isn't awaiting you.

I know it sounds cliché.
"You don't understand."
"What do you know about my pain?"

You're right, maybe I don't know about your pain, but what I do know is that you've already given so much of yourself to your past. I have experienced heartbreak, mental instability, betrayal, death, debt, and abuse. We all walk a path of darkness within our lives and sometimes that darkness happens to weigh on ourselves and others. I could tell you of my scars. I can show you my scars, but maybe I'm just like you keeping it all in. Scared of what the world would think if my demons became public domain. So sometimes we pretend we're fine trying to make it through fighting a past that tries to consume us daily. I can't blame you because I'd have to blame me too. For some days my life lives to another sunrise but I'm empty inside. Memories prey on my vulnerability dragging me back to a time where depression had me within its grasp.

We must remember that our past doesn't define us. It's not about who we were, but to mold us into who we are. We can't change the person in the past or the hurt, but we can work on the present, so the future holds a different outcome. Again, not saying it's easy, because God knows it's far from it. Impossible? No! Let's make the steps to be better. Why not walk it together? I'd love to have you come along. It's time we reunite with happiness we've kept waiting for too long!

Letting Go and Self-Worth

Burdened by the interrogation of self-identity, untying the knots and strands of who and what composes this mind, body, and soul. Finding wounds and splinters that have dry rotted all sense of direction and purpose, but the truth is:

I am not who I was.
I am not what I've done.
I am who I become.
I am becoming!
I am healing.
I am forgiveness.
I will never be the same as I was,
And I rejoice in that knowing.
I am becoming!
And I'm more than ok with that.

Letting go of the past may be one of the hardest tasks you'll ever have to do. You'll have to open old wounds and scars to address them. However, letting it out is crucial to your growth. You may not understand why you had to experience some things, but it was all apart of the process. It's not about being superhuman and defeating every obstacle. It's about the exact opposite, enduring hardships and overcoming them. It's about being brave enough to walk away and live on. In saying that, I may not know your story and you may not know mine but believe in the purpose over your life because nothing can stop you. Sometimes we hold on to the past by living what seems to be a nightmare. We lose sight of who we are on the inside and we ignore the positive life has to offer.

Sure, when you've been in the dark for so long it's hard to see outside of your circumstances. However, having a little hope can help you reach the light. Hope is a choice. It's a state of mind in which we must choose to be present. I've walked alone in the dark for years. Feeling unloved and unworthy of achieving more because I allowed my past to control my future. Although I was in a dark place, I still had hope. Sometimes we need support and encouragement from others to pull us through. Never give up on hope. Keep the faith knowing that you can overcome whatever battle. Faith isn't about asking God to stop the storm. It's about trusting God to help you through it! Keep all your trust in God. He will get you through any storm. You aren't alone. There is someone out there battling the same storm. Let my words be the helping hand you need to make your world brighter!

Freedom And Mental Healeth

What you don't see are the tears at night. The insecurities weighing upon her self-esteem. Her fears and doubts, her heartache and pain. Anxiety stifling her breath and hijacking any moment of peace she clings to. What you don't hear are the screams within her mind, begging for help but too afraid of being judged to speak. The voices constantly breaking her down, telling her she's not enough, she's to blame, and she isn't worth it! The prayers to God asking for deliverance. You may see her beauty and feel the warmth of her smile but not the storm brewing within her. She's crying for help, but no one hears. She's crying for help, but society is cruel to mental instability. There's many like her, right beside you, at your job, in your class, and at home. Mental health is real and so is her struggle. Be the change she needs, the ear for her voice, and the hand to help her up. We're all on this journey together!

I hope you will release. I'd like you to be free. Let the chains fall from your wrist so you may fully breathe. There is a sort of love that exist above the earth. It's connected to your past. It has zero material worth, but with it you are royalty. You are the child of The King. You're grounded down to spread this love but to grievance you cling. Clear them all away and feel the color white. Dissolve the rest because it's for the best. Have clarity in your sight. Ground your feet down. Look straight ahead, head high and shoulders back. Turn pain into beauty and vulnerability into strength. Persistence is an asset to withstand the length.

Free

*I*believe the reality of life is this, we all just want to be free. The questions that I fathom myself and maybe you do too. Are we searching for something that can never be? Have we really escaped our past? Have we escaped the pain? Are we just pretending like we're okay or have we really been changed? Have we really been healed? Have we really found peace? Because even with my prayers I still can't seem to find sleep. These silent battles are killing me. Lord, I just wanna be free! I search for purpose, and it seems like the search is worthless. Honestly, I fear the body of Christ because I'm more judged by people in churches than in the streets.

They expect me to be perfect, but that's a cross that I can't carry. My soul still battles with sin. Does it make me less christian if I told you, sometimes I struggle to believe when I say amen? Maybe it's just me or maybe I'm the only one who'll admit it. It's crazy how the ones you love most support you the least and turn out to be your biggest critics. They come to me for answers when I have so many questions. My life is so numb by pain that it's hard for me to feel blessings. Lord, I just wanna be free! I'm tired of painting pictures of perfection. I'm tired of being enslaved to my fear. I wanna believe I'm here for a reason but sometimes that reason isn't clear. It's hard for me to move forward because I can't help but think my next step is where my feet will fail. Lord, I feel trapped in a prison and my mind is the cell. I just wanna be free! Speak to me, Lord.

I need to hear your voice because it's times like this when I feel like death is the only choice. Death can be gain but death brings pain and pain brings change. I don't want to stay the same. I wanna be free! Maybe I will be free when I decide it's more you and less me, Lord. Maybe I will be free when I finally understand your purpose is greater than my dreams. Maybe I will be free when I stop pleasing opinions and start pleasing you! Maybe I will be free when I stop embracing lies and start embracing truth! Maybe I will be free when I stop searching for myself in the world and discover everything that you made me to be! Maybe I will be free when I get out my own way and follow your path! Maybe I will be free when I stop searching for something I already have! I just want to be free! Maybe, just maybe, I already free!

The broken are the most beautiful because they have known darkness. They know the joy of finally having the light warm them again. Rebuilding themselves one piece at a time. Slowly and painfully putting it all together again. Also remembering their cracks are what keep the dark at bay. For these imperfections are what allow the light to come within. The broken have such shining souls for they've learned that's where true love and happiness come from. You must give from your soul to truly be able to receive. They most fervently wish for no one else to shatter and break as they have. The broken are brave and have warrior hearts. They know how to claw their way out of darkness and how to help those that are falling. They are not afraid for they have faced the unfathomable and survived. Bravery is relative.

For some, it exists on the corners of the world starving and fighting. For others, it exists on the properties of mankind protecting and helping. The bravery I know is the one that lives inside me because I am my very first battleground. My thoughts never fall asleep, and I let them be. To not allow them to speak what may be wrong or obscene, might not be so. If you look in deep, this is what I know. Then I remember that my ideas are wrong for me. I felt isolated on my battlefield. It was me fighting my world as if it was my enemy.

One fine morning I looked in the mirror and smiled at myself. I embrace myself and now the world embraces me too. We are all unique and made to be different. Don't allow anyone to tell you who you should be. You were meant to be unique and like no other. In this society everyone thinks they have to fit into societal norms. Wrong! Step outside of what everyone else is doing and be you. Don't try to fit into what society says you must be! In your suffering seek deeper mindfulness which is the awareness of what precious part of you calls out for healing by screaming emotions. Approach the constellation of you being with loving curiosity hoping to encounter that which was hidden in the shadows blinding you to yourself, all of you. You can see how to serve, accept, and understand.

In God's presence, you are graced with the vision of the path forward. It is with deep gratitude and humility that you'll live as it will rescue you from the depths of despair and existential crisis. I no longer fear suffering but welcome it with joy as an opportunity to become deeper and truer. By pushing suffering away and trying to avoid what was coming, I did myself a great disservice. I kept myself blind unknowingly feeding my past, hoping for freedom. In embracing it, you'll find the love and joy. You are the medicine that can heal the hurt!

Dear Self,

I know it's hard to move forward some days because you get trapped in the flashbacks of your pain. You feel like you're drowning and running out of air. You feel paralyzed and unable to move or speak. The guilt and shame consume you and worst of all you struggle with trusting people. Therefore, most days you suffer in silence. Here's a rose for you today. For all the times you were about to give up but didn't. For each day that you pulled yourself out of the battles with depression and sadness.

The fact that you're still pushing through pain and overcoming life obstacles, I salute you and I'm proud of you. I know it's not easy and your perseverance is amazing! Better days are coming. May you find peace in the promise of the solstice night, that each day forward is blessed with more light. That the cycle of nature, unbroken and true brings faith to your soul and well being to you. From the darkness comes light! Time for personal awakening and inner work. This is the time to break generational curses and deal with past traumas that hold us back. It's time to focus on changing toxic patterns, stop living in the past. It was a lesson, not a life sentence. It is time to reflect and recreate yourself!

It was self-preservation that kept her heart and mind oceans apart. But it was God who turned the pain into a symphony of healing and created beauty of her scars. If we do nothing else in this life let's give hope to the hopeless. Be a light to those who are lost in weariness. A friend who expects absolutely nothing in return and with boldness show our imperfections and scars. My friends, even when it's hard allowed people to see what God does with the impossible!!

The Flight

*I*t takes strength to smile in the face of hurt. Not everyone can hide the pain and act like everything is all fine. Behind closed doors the tears and thoughts run rampant consuming your mind. Just continue being strong, even when it takes all that's within you to simply function. The day will appear when that smile will be genuine, and the tears won't be those of pain but of joy and happiness. It's such a sad thing that we hear I love you so often around us in the world but see so little of it outside the words. People seem to use love to manipulate for their personal gain rather than to represent the magic that it truly is.

Fight is defined as the contend in battle or physical combat to put forth a determined effort. When we hear the word fight, we usually think of chaos between two or more parties. In this case, I'm referring to fighting within yourself and for your life. The fight can be against demons within you or your past. You must fight! Giving up is the easiest decision you can make but fighting shows courage and strength! So, fighting to beat whatever is holding you back from being all that you can and will be.

It is worth it in the end. In my own life I've also struggled with fighting plenty of battles inside myself, which includes all the pain from childhood, addiction, shame, guilt, and thinking that I wasn't worthy of anything. Pushing through those events got me to look inside myself and see something better. So, when you question yourself and ask is it really worth it, the answer is yes. It's worth it because you will be better as the result. People will look at your life and be inspired. They will say since you did it, they can too! So be that example for the world and let them know that the past didn't control your future.

The Life in Death

I read a poem about death, and it made me believe in truth. Every time I think I am going to die, It's true. One day I am going to be dead, that's the truth of the story. My flesh is going to be decomposing or recomposing itself in a future form of life. Whether it be an apple seed sprouting or an elephant being birth in the planes of Africa, death is true. So, it's intriguing how something like death can spark a profound perspective. On the inverse, it's when life gets ugly that I appreciate it's beauty. When the pain is almost crippling, I find myself holding more and more adoration and respect for those who have been through hell and still believe in heaven on an intimate level. In reading this many could think that this is about physically dying, but in retrospect, could you see it in another light?

Can you see yourself emotionally and mentally dying in an instance? Life sometimes forces everything you ever knew to die, to create something you were already destined to be. Sometimes it may seem that you were born into a world that would be filled with nothing but pain because that's all you knew from the start. Sometimes that can be so haunting that you find yourself fighting it so hard that it destroys you to a point that you have nothing but faith to hold onto. When you're down to your lowest fight, drowning in so many emotions all you want is silence.

Oh, but then you begin to actually feel everything in every way. Oh yes, sometimes that can feel very heavy, but sometimes parts of you have to die so that you can live! Whether that's pain and suffering or things you hold onto because it cut so deep that it's hard for you to see past it. That's what the fight is for, for God to recreate you into who he knows you to be! Death can be a tricky subject but it's far past physical so let go of who you knew yourself to be and fight for who you're destined to be!

She didn't give up.
She gave into the beauty of unconditional surrender
and the profound that exudes forth from the movement of
vulnerability.
She didn't give up. She gave into all that was confounding her
and breathed it in for all it was worth.
In turn her exhales became contagious.
For the power that pulls when conditions are null,
 the walls of expectation lay prostrate.
Surrender will be no where near the shores of giving up,
but rather within the foundation of wisdom and understanding.
That's why she didn't give up,
but surrendered.

She won!!
The undoing of her surrender
captivated what tied and bind her.
She relinquished all she had reserved to find pieces of her she

didn't even know she had.
In the stripping of everything she ever thought she was,
she raised hands and without speaking her silence broke!
Her raised hands made all her broken dreams evoke!

Loss of sight,
yet unseen senses fight to break ground.
Vision blurred,
but insight beyond clarity she has found.
Waves of hope and tsunamis of questions crash upon levies shores
of her heart.

Yet she defines her perspective even when definition and depth
perception have her tripping over her thoughts, words, and any
direction that resembles a sliver of survival.
Although her countenance may wane and her moments grows
heavy,
She is beauty!
She is worthy!
She is admirable beyond question.

For she fights not for sight
and she labors not for a vision of the future,
but she loves for the sake of fighting what most would deem a lost
call.

She loves for the sake of passing on a torch of hope to the
generations beyond her that will find themselves in even darker
places than where she found herself.
She holds insight that most eyes wouldn't even believe if laid
before them and organized alphabetically.
She gives even hope a reason to believe in itself.
She is beauty because she continued to fight!

You have been burdened! You've been pained! You've had days

where you felt you were going insane! You're enduring trials and tribulations. You've seen the lowest places of life. You've been kicked around, and you've been burned, enduring the scars of tragedy and still yet still, you're here breathing!

There is a power residing inside of you! There is a strong force living inside of you! Are you prepared to fight for your life like it's worth fighting for?

Where are you at? It's time to give birth to your warrior because in this season you are about to receive everything that was taken from you and more!

Rise up and claim your power. Break barriers and crush chains! Break generational curses! Break away from limited thinking and inferiority mentality! Those struggles, your past, and your current situation don't define you!

Break free from the trauma, anxiety, depression, fear, and shame. Keep fighting for your life. Keep getting back up after you fall! You are breaking free from the chains of bondage!!

Restoration / Healing

A smile wipes away thousands of tears. Who knows what hides behind it? He who has suffered the time, only that one knows reality of time. It wasn't shame that broke you! It wasn't words that stole you! It wasn't naming that hurt you! It was yourself agreeing that nothing could restore you!

A yawning gulf between my vision tree and my reality plant. A yawning gulf between the place I love to live and the place I live. I love to live under the vault of heaven. Alas my existence lives! In the valley of the shadow of death, peace has escaped my remembrance. I know a swing of the pendulum will change my face and fate. My surrender supreme shall marry my dream boat with my reality shore. After dark night comes the shining bright morning. Look at the dismal side of your life and you'll feel like you're living the darkest of them all. Oh, now wait! Just wait for a second. Turn over the page and ponder over the positive side of your state. You'll eventually realize that you're living the brightest life of all in this sphere! You've pushed through the storms and dark clouds and found a reason to smile! People are looking at you and wondering how you made it through when everyone counted you out.

You made it! You wake up every morning and do what you must do. You endure every struggle that life has thrown your way. You're the precious gem that others may have thrown away and didn't think twice about it. Oh, but now they wish they never did! So, smile love, even on the darkest day. Smile because you've made it further than what they expected. God is restoring everything that you lost fighting through what most would have considered to be the end for you. Times I felt like giving up and there were nights no one was around. All I had was me. I've felt the feeling of being unloved and not wanted. Not saying that it's okay, but no matter how alone you may feel, you're never really alone! Sometimes there won't be people around to tell you to keep going, so you must encourage yourself. Trust God to help push you to keep going!

I believe in impossible dreams.
I believe in miracles too.
I believe you can accomplish anything.
I believe in YOU.
I believe the sky is the limit.
I believe the stars are in your reach.
I believe life's what you make it.

So, learn, so you can teach.
Stand up and be the boss of your destiny!
All you need is already in you.
Be everything you are meant to be.
Open your ears and hear.
Open your eyes and see.
Believe in dreams because dreams believe in you.

Never let your dreams fade away.
Keep stepping forward because you'll make it through.
Sometimes you will fall.
Get right back up! Be strong and don't give up.
Give it your best shot. Give it your all.
Whether you win or lose,
it's up to you. It's your call.
Victory is your destiny and greatness is your anatomy!

I've learned that there is more to your struggles than just surviving.
I've learned that storms are what we prepare, uproot, and turn
soil for growth to bloom. There are lessons to be breathed in every
inhale. However difficult or shallow the breathes may feel, there
will be pain and gasping on the exhale. But I've learned there
is more to struggling than just surviving. Struggle prepares the
pages for gratitude to be written on the foundation of your heart's
narrative.

Healing trauma is hard. It's the back and forward learning,
unlearning, getting up, falling back down, working through anxiety
and depression, feeling alone, then pushing people away. Being
confused, feeling misunderstood, not understanding yourself,
dealing with negative thoughts, struggling with unhealthy coping
habits, feeling ashamed and the list goes on.

But it's something about the idea that one day, life will be better
that keeps me going. It's something about knowing that I'm
breaking generational curses that keep me pushing forward. It's
something inside me that drives me to try once more each day I
wake up.

True enough, we get tired. Many days you want to quit, but for
some reason, you can't. You can't leave yourself hanging like that.

In the battle for your healing, you need to know that the inner critic will not give up without a fight. Understand that you are going up against thoughts that have crippled you for years. Thoughts that have tried to keep you in the bondage of your pain. You're going up against thoughts of helplessness and worthlessness and maybe even depression or suicide.

As I've said repeatedly fighting back is not going to be easy. Reclaiming your life will not come passively because this pain was designed to destroy you. Thinking it will be easy is going to set you up for heartbreaking disappointment.

The truth is, there are times where you will feel like there's no hope for you. But in these moments, you must learn how to think and recognize deceit. Some of our thoughts were shaped through pain, and this causes us to get deceived in certain areas of life. We start to believe we are hopeless victims that can't heal or become whole.

Assuming we must accept the life of mediocrity is the trick of the enemy. It's an absolute lie to receive!!

You may get punched by shame, negative voices, fear, and discouragement on many days, but you cannot stay down. You can not quit on yourself. You can not give up on yourself because you are worth fighting for even if you do not believe. You owe it to yourself to see what the wholeness version of you looks like.

You are tougher than you know. After all, you survived the fire this far! So don't let pain deceive you into believing you're weak and helpless. Fight back with truth! Fight back by taking care of yourself even when you feel undeserving! Fight with all the force inside of you!

Now more than ever is when you need to accept love and support from genuine people. Now more than ever is when you need to educate yourself on trauma and its effects on your life. Now is the time to take your life back!

Understand this: A traumatic past does NOT, will NOT, ever ever ever get to define your future. So gracefully pick yourself up, heal, and try again!

The hands of time grabbed my heart, and in that moment, knowing I had no control of turning back the clock, I spoke to the future and told her she was mine.

So, pour me another glass of walls. Let them run down the corridors of my soul.
Building foundation of separation from all that has ever tried to stand against me. But what really does another wall gain you besides a perch to stand upon and boast of your bitterness. So, pour me another glass of walls. Let me drink them down, digesting all they are made of and let the waste flow from my soul. For never again will I take part in destruction of building walls around me. Let walls fall. Let healing build you. Let the scabs become scars you look upon to remind you of where you refuse to stay. Let growth be your everyday direction to bring you restoration!

Textured Emotions

*T*ears textured the pages she wrote, and her emotions bled ink into the paper's fiber. Her heart sank into the depth of her expression and her tears would swallow a sea of words, while her heart bled them for all to read. Can you look beyond the physical? I mean really see inside one's soul. To reach all the broken pieces and view all the stories untold. The strong person you see on the outside.

The one that always says everything's okay, but deep down their drowning just waiting for someone to care enough to read every page. Every moment of sadness! Every bit of fear! Would you be able to see their silent tears? Emotions can run deep as you allow them but sometimes it's best to leave them exactly where you found them! My heart cries out for every soul that's lost and searching for the place they can call home because living in a deep hole you built inside yourself sometimes can make you feel alone.

I hear people say they must find their selves but finding yourself is not really how it works! You aren't a ten-dollar bill in last winters coat pocket! You are also not lost! Your true self is right there buried under culture conditioning, other people's opinions, and inaccurate conclusions you drew as a child that became your beliefs about who you are!

Finding yourself is actually returning to yourself, unlearning, excavation, and remembering who you were before the world got its hands on you. So, everyday choose life! Every morning, wake up and choose joy! Choose to feel the freedom that comes from being able to make choices! Today, choose to feel life. Don't deny your humanity but embrace it! Let it go and be who you were destined to be!
If there is a future, it's a time for mending. Time to see your troubles coming to an ending.

Life is never hopeless however great your sorrow if you're looking forward to a new tomorrow. If there's a time for wishing, there is a time for hoping. When found in darkness you are blindly groping. Though the heart be heavy and hurt you may be feeling. If there's a time for praying, there is time for healing. Through your window there is a new day breaking. Thank God for the promise though the mind and soul be aching. If with harvest over there is grain enough for gleaning, there is a new tomorrow.

Your life still has meaning!

Forgiveness / Love:

Trading Hearts

I no longer feel anything. Can you relate? A broke person would love to trade places with a millionaire. But would you be willing to trade hearts with a hurt person? Where every part of you has been revealed. That numb feeling you get when you can't feel your fingers in the brisk cold. Your feelings aren't present, but you talk about being emotional. You are emotionless. Would you be willing to trade your perfectly cold heart for a warm one? One that seeks love. Would you trade your heart for a broken one?

To see how pain feels, would you be able to trade hearts with a person that's been through hell? Could you hear the thought? Could you take the flame? Would you trade hearts with a person that has that desire and that fire to find a love that stays hidden? Would you be willing to trade hearts with someone that would give their heart to someone else? Just for a false feeling of happiness. You wouldn't because you wouldn't trade a life of no feeling for a life of overwhelming emotion. You wouldn't trade your loveless existence for a life full of joy. Although I despise it, I admire it after all. Who would trade numbness? For an abundance of external wounds.

To the person reading this who has experienced a traumatic childhood, broken heart, or any kind of pain.
There will come a time in this life when you will have realized you were treated indirectly or directly wrong or exposed to things that you shouldn't have been exposed to in childhood, in which such exposure has impacted you negatively.

You deserve to receive closure and an apology for the pain that you endured. Unfortunately, you may never receive one externally. The question then is, will self remain in a sunken place at the mercy of hoping to receive and apology or an explanation from another soul? Or will you give self everything that you need and deserve now? Even if it's an apology for things that you didn't personally do?
Instead of helplessly holding our hand out, waiting for another soul to heal or save us, I've learned that we each possess the power to heal and pour life into ourselves. As adults, we can nurture our spirits and give self the things we never received but so desperately deserved. This includes apologies, love, security, compassion, freedom, grace, and permission to move forward. It may take time and practice before these things arrive, but that's perfectly okay!

Are you ready to reclaim your inner power and take responsibility for self? Are you willing to be the voice that you need to guide your soul to wholeness? Thoughts for yourself: I know whose to blame. I know what's the source of my pain. Now I need to know whose job is it to fix me?

The answer is, it's the person who stares back at you when you look in the mirror.

Forgiveness is the intentional or voluntary process by which a victim undergoes a change in feelings and attitude regarding an offense. We must let go of negative emotions such as vengefulness. Forgiveness is another hard step that you must take especially after being hurt by people who say they care about you. We tend to hold grudges or hurt and pain that was caused by someone we care about. In this process on growing and moving on pass storms you must forgive.

You are Enough

*T*o be worthy means to be a person notable or important in a particular sphere. Good enough and suitable you are.

I am not sure how you felt when you first begin to read this book but let this serve as a reminder that you are worthy and valuable. You are worth more than any external thing in this world, and your identity cannot be defined nor duplicated. You are more than your mistakes. You are more than your fears. You are more than the pain in your heart. You are more than self esteem issues and insecurity. The trials of life can make us vulnerable to believing the lie that we are not good enough, not pretty enough, not smart enough! The truth is you are more than enough. The fact that you are breathing right now makes you a human worth living for.

I pray these pages brings you many blessings and reminders of your worth. Understand your worth is not attached to how you feel or think, not a life experience, nor the words that another says. Your worth comes from the divine source that resides inside of you! And this means you are intentionally designed for this present moment! You are royalty and don't you ever forget that!

Own Your Story!
Own Your Truth!
Own Your Life!

*T*here is power in your story. There is power in your truth. There is healing found in owning everything that represents you, the good, the bad, the past, and the present. You see, life can throw you curveballs. Life can back us into scary corners. Life can have a way of silencing us in the pit of pain and sorrow. Then there are people. The ones that bleed on other people. The ones that hurt other people. The ones that traumatize other people. The people who cause pain but take no responsibility. Then there is you.

Are you somewhere hiding in your shame? Are you somewhere suffering in silence? Are you trying to keep it all together but feel as if you're falling apart? Where are you today? Do you know what experiences shaped you into who you are now? Does it paralyze you to think about situations from the past? Back then everything may not have been all good. And if we're being honest, some of the bad may have outweighed the good. Some of the bad may still be causing problems in your life today. So, you must decide if you will face your truth or let the past devour your life!

Owning your story and your truth will free you from that piercing pain that lives inside. The key word is your story and your truth. Not the watered-down version that hides your heart. Not the downplayed version that others may have forced you to believe! But the facts about how you have been shaped, scarred, and carried by life!

When I say your story, I mean finding your voice and acknowledging your inner pain. Does it hurt to acknowledge your truth? Do shame and guilt follow? Have you been manipulated into believing your truth isn't true?

Let me tell you something! No one, absolutely no one, can tell you how to feel about anything that you experienced! Your feelings are real. Your truth is your truth. And no one can own your truth but you.

Beautiful soul, step into the light. Let's free self from the silent game because that holds self captive. And we can not afford to be weighed down by the baggage of shame. Silence cripples us. Owning our story frees us. Understand this, your life story made you stronger.
Your life story made you unique. Own it! Look it in the eyes! Walk through it. Then, when you've learned all you can learn, heal and rise above that chapter in your book!

Claim your power!

Abiding in a State of Peace & Understanding

*I*know there are times you feel totally empty, as though you have nothing left to give whatsoever. I know you feel weak, tired, helpless, and overwhelmed. The emotions and thoughts you have within, I know them well. I am more than acquainted with these sentiments, but even still let me remind you God is greater than these things. Things will come and surely you will encounter testing times. You will experience a number of tests, but God's grace will get you through. God has so much stored up for you that you can not even fathom. He has expanded your capacity even further than you previously perceived.

He has expanded you wider, higher, and deeper than you have noticed. With the awakening to this reality, your perception and interpretation of present difficulties will change. You will see your problems are truly small. You will see your light as momentary afflicted. No longer investing and believing the afflictions have power and permanence in your life. You will walk in the light and discover there is no darkness in you. He is filling your mind with thoughts of hope and vision of your future. He is filling your heart with emotions of joy, hope, peace, and love. He is filling your circumstances with his presence which pours out fullness of joy! Do not continue to settle for less than what has already been given to you. Adopt the full spectrum for what He has for you. I am telling you in this moment, although you may experience hardship and resistance, rest assured you will overcome them all! You will not only understand your position, but you will also apprehend and manifest it too.

Expect as you walk with faith that your life will continue to change as you grow. Tomorrow will turn out differently than yesterday, and the hope of tomorrow will not disappoint you. God will show you what you possess. He will show you reality that is beyond what your eyes have seen, your ears have heard, or your mind has conceived. It will shift your focus to what is long lasting and eternal. In this way you will understand and appreciate your present position today, knowing better who you are, and where you are going. You will abide in a state of peace and understanding, no longer floundering in confusion and disappointment.

So, allow yourself to continue to be brave and have peace.
It is brave that you get up in the mornings when your heart aches, life is messy, and you do not feel like being in the world.
It is brave that you continue to love, express, and open your soul despite the way you were treated in the past. I think it's brave that you keep believing in something more or bigger even when you may not know what you are hoping for. It's brave that you fight and choose to move forward. That is what makes you strong!